Mel Bay Presents

TWIN Fiddling

By Stacy Phillips

D1609011

CD CONTENTS:

1 Introduction (1:13)	18 Old Joe Clark (:30)	35 Tableau Clog Dance (:38)	50 Joys of Wedlock (:28)
2 Bill Cheatem (:29)	19 Red Haired Boy (:30)	36 Tombigbee Waltz (:50)	51 Thompson's Jig (:27)
3 Brilliance (:42)	20 Texas Quick Step (:29)	37 Wayfaring Stranger (1:06)	52 Tobin's Jig (:28)
4 Cindy (:27)	21 Turkey in the Straw (:27)	38 Careless Love (:30)	53 Bully of the Town (:38)
5 Cobbler's Reel (:27)	22 Two Friends Quadrille (:41)	39 In the Pines (:18)	54 Gran Texas (:26)
6 Cotton Eyed Joe (:44)	23 Weave and Way (:29)	40 Little Maggie (:28)	55 Jesse Polka (:50)
7 Did You Ever See the Devil Uncle Joe? (:32)	24 Woodchopper's Reel (:28)	41 R.K. Special (:53)	56 Peor Es Nada (1:37)
8 Fire on the Mountain (:32)	25 Danish Waltz (:38)	42 Sitting on Top of the World (bluegrass version) (:26)	57 Rainbow (:48)
9 Golden Slippers (:49)	26 Finnish Waltz (:51)		58 Redwing (:43)
10 Goodbye Liza Jane (:28)	27 Homecoming Waltz (1:22)	43 Train 45 (:25)	59 Silver Bells (:44)
11 Harvest Home Hornpipe (:38)	28 Memory Waltz (1:54)	44 Watermelon on the Vine (:42)	60 Snow Deer (:45)
12 June Apple (:29)	29 Norwegian Waltz (1:09)	45 Bishop of Bangor (:27)	61 Spanish Two Step (:45)
13 La Cassine Special (:31)	30 Old Madeira Waltz (:44)	46 Black Nag (:28)	62 Stealing Home (:53)
14 Liberty (:29)	31 Si Bheag Si Mhor (:52)	47 The Connaughtman's Rambles (:28)	63 Taking Off (:58)
15 Muddy Roads (:29)	32 Sitting On Top of the World (blues version) (:24)		64 Washington and Lee Swing (:40)
16 Old French (:30)	33 Star of the County Down (:56)	48 Cowboy Jig (:28)	65 Year of the Jubilo (:29)
17 Old Jaw Bone (:24)	34 Swedish Walking Tune (:58)	49 The Irish Washerwoman (:28)	66 Conclusion (:55)

Stacy Phillips – fiddle • Dave Howard – guitar • Marty Laster – occasional harmony fiddle
Billy Sherr – engineer at Jack Straw Studios, New Haven, CT.

Visit us on the Web at http://www.melbay.com — E-mail us at email@melbay.com

1 2 3 4 5 6 7 8 9 0

Table of Contents

Introduction

Most fiddle music is meant to be played with others. It is not uncommon for three or four fiddlers, along with five string banjos, guitars and mandolins in an old-time music jam session to play the same tune for fifteen to thirty minutes. Fiddlers that favor Celtic music will usually play medleys with bevies of fiddlers, plectrum banjos, accordions, guitars, penny whistles, and flutes. These two styles of musicians play the tunes in unison with almost no exceptions.

Harmony fiddles were a mainstay of western swing groups almost from its inception. Cecil Brower and Cliff Bruner played with the first great band, Milton Brown and the Musical Brownies. The Bob Wills and Spade Cooley bands often carried three fiddlers.

This approach was adopted by the popular groups of early commercial country music. Throughout the 1950's and part of the 60's much of the recorded output of Nashville featured multiple fiddles. Players like Dale Potter and Buddy Spicher specialized in playing double stop (i.e. two strings at a time) harmonies to the lead lines of other studio musicians, notably Tommy Jackson.

Bill Monroe also used double and even triple fiddles in his bluegrass groups when he could afford to hire the extra musicians. This fiddling is a combination of old time, blues, a bit of swing and a large infusion of the commercial country styles of the 1940's and 50's. Bobby Hicks, Vassar Clements and Kenny Baker contributed to the classic fiddle duets and trios sound of The Blue Grass Boys. I have decided that it is time for old-time and Celtic fiddlers to join their swing and bluegrass brethren in the cheerful world of twin fiddling.

This selection of harmonized tunes is culled from several genres. The largest group is traditional southern fiddle tunes, but there are many northern, Canadian and British entries. I think that jigs are a fertile, as yet untapped field for harmony, and so have included a separate section of them. On the other hand waltzes have always been the prime target for broadsides of multiple fiddles. There are two obvious reasons. They are slow, so the harmony need not be as technically demanding as in a breakdown. Secondly, because they are slow, shortcomings of pitch and tone are more apparent than in fast numbers. Adding a second violin often makes both players sound smoother. (That is one reason for having masses of violinists in orchestra.) There are also several swing numbers, blues, rags, and a section of bluegrass numbers.

The entries are alphabetized and not in order of difficulty. In fact, the first couple of tunes are among the most challenging in the book. Don't panic. Have courage. There are plenty of easy ones.

I have arranged the harmonies to minimize technical demands, but you must eventually face the task of reaching for the heights of second and third positions. As with any new chore, the key is to get it right slowly before increasing the tempo. If you cannot handle upper positions just play the difficult parts an octave lower (so that they will sound below the melody). Occasionally a bit of the melody has been altered from the "standard" version for the sake of easier and/or more interesting harmonies.

The accompanying recording should ease the learning process. The melody and harmony are in separate channels in your stereo so you can do the "music-minus-one" shtick. Most of the selections are played slowly to let you join in as soon as possible. Dave Howard supplied the guitar rhythm and fiddle ace Marty Laster played harmony on "Bill Cheatem," "Brilliance," "Did You Ever See the Devil," "Fire on the Mountain," "June Apple," "Old Jaw Bone," "Old Joe Clark," "Red Haired Boy," "Weave and Way," "Woodchopper's Reel," "Memory Waltz," "Wayfaring Stranger," "Sitting on Top of the World" (bluegrass version), "Train 45," "Bishop of Bangor," "Thompson's Jig," "Peor Es Nada," "Stealing Home," and "Taking Off."

As I just mentioned, adding fiddlers can mask some intonation problems, but this ploy cannot make them disappear. The final 10% or so of in-tuneness can be the difference between just getting through a tune and the joy of consonant harmonies that reverberate through your whole body as well as the room in which you play. This warning is just a lead-in to the usual teacher's admonition to make sure you can play it slowly before taking off.

The ultimate purpose of this book is to give you the ability to make up your own harmonies. I have employed different approaches to similar situations so that you can decide which you favor. The "Basic Music Theory" appendix should help you to understand how I determined my choices of notes. And now - *en garde* with your bows. Prepare to enter the sensuous world of harmonies sweet and hot.

Stacy Phillips
January 1995

Interpreting The Notation

Most of the music notation in this book is standard. I have included a few special symbols which are particularly useful for fiddling.

In general, *bowing has been left to you*. Most of the pieces are notated with saw strokes (i.e. one note per bow) by default. You should have a general knowledge of the types of phrasing that differentiate old time, bluegrass, British and swing fiddling. Bow patterns, and the lack thereof are very important to getting the correct feel for a tune. Certainly all triplets should be slurred in American tunes. This is often not the case in Celtic music. Canadian players use very little slurring, especially when compared to Southeastern old-timers. Bluegrass and swing fiddlers tend to lie between the extremes. The range of acceptable phrasing is enormous and this book is not the proper forum. Refer to the listings in "Other Books of Interest" for some texts that deal with this subject.

I occasionally refer to "single shuffle" or "Georgia bow". Theses are rhythmic bow patterns designed to give an accent on third and/or seventh 1/8 note in a measure. Note that the Georgia bow slurs all the notes but the accented ones.

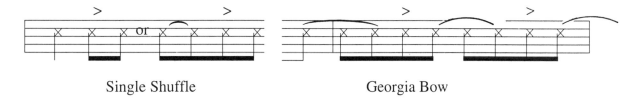

Single Shuffle   Georgia Bow

All notes included under a slur should be played without change in bow direction. Synchronized bowing makes for maximum sleekness and blend with multiple fiddlers.

There are two notations for slides. In either case, do not change fingering or bow direction.

a) A jagged line between two notes indicates a slide from the first up or down to the second. These glissandi are usually quick, but taking time away from the first or second note to allow a relatively slow move is certainly acceptable. In general, however, both notes should sound for the indicated durations. The speed of the slide and which note of the two should lose time to the slide is up to you.

b) A diagonal line to or from a note head indicates a short (usually not more than a half-step) quick slide. *The pitch at the beginning of the slide has no duration.* (This is opposed to the diagonal symbol, described above.) Your finger should be moving even as it hits the string.

The capital letters above the staves are chordal accompaniment. The small numbers in parentheses over the staves are recommended fingering.

OLD TIME FIDDLE TUNES

BILL CHEATEM *(melody)*

This number is a standard in both the old time and bluegrass worlds. Apparently Arthur Smith, an important fiddler in the 1930's and '40's was the person who made it well known. The harmony has a couple of quick, challenging shifts to third position.

BILL CHEATEM (*harmony*)

Bill Monroe and the Blue Grass Boys in Pennsylvania in 1970. Left to right: Kenny Baker, Joe Stuart, Rual Yarborough, Bill Monroe, James Monroe and Skip Payne. (photo: Carl Fleischauer)

BRILLIANCE *(melody)*

The melody is actually a couple of old hornpipes pasted together by Howdy Forrester. The harmony is my responsibility. This is one of the tougher arrangements in this book. The melody can serve as a challenging etude for any violinist. Good luck.

BRILLIANCE *(harmony)*

CINDY *(melody)*

"Cindy got religion,
She had it once before,
But when she hears my old banjo,
She's the first one on the floor.

Get along home, home Cindy, get along home I say,
Get along home, home Cindy, I'll marry you someday."

Them's pretty racy lyrics for a fiddle tune. There has always been a tug of war between the anti-frivolity stance of old-time religion in the mountains of America's southeast and the love of the secular dance music traditional to that area. Check out the typical repertoire of the old bluegrass bands, with honky tonk and gospel tunes played in the same set.

CINDY *(harmony)*

Tony Trischka, Kenny Kosek, Stacy Phillips and Dede Wyland breaking down "Ralph's Banjo Special" at a concert in Sydney, Australia ca. 1980. Kenny is a very in-demand studio fiddler in New York City. You have heard his unidentified efforts on countless commercials. (photo: Stacy Phillips collection)

COBBLER'S REEL (melody)

The harmony for this Canadian tune also works well an octave lower in section one. In the next to last measure of that section the third from last note of the melody was changed from B to C to allow an open E in the harmony. This provides a convenient moment to change hand positions. Up to that point the harmony in the first section can be played entirely in third position.

At the end of measure 4 of the first section I chose a G in the harmony though F♯ would fit the chord better. This is because the other times this part of the melody appears it is over a G chord and the ear becomes accustomed to the G/D harmony. Plus, a G chord follows immediately.

Many people know this tune by the enigmatic title "You Married My Daughter But You Didn't." An interpretation of this declaration would be welcomed by the author.

COBBLER'S REEL (harmony)

6

COTTON EYED JOE (melody)

This is one of several tunes with the same name. There is an infamous line dance in the world of commercial country music that is connected with this version. The first eight measures are a tempo-setting introduction, with the harmony laying out for the first two. Alternative settings of the first section are presented with identical second sections. J.R.Chatwell, the great western swing fiddler, was the first to record this.

You can opt to only play the upper notes of the double stops in the body of this tune's harmony.

The last two measures are a standard fiddle tune tag.

COTTON EYED JOE (harmony)

DID YOU EVER SEE THE DEVIL UNCLE JOE? *(melody)*

This tune is also known as "Hop Light Ladies" and "Miss McLeod's Reel." It works well with some shuffle bowing. The difficult moment is the shift necessary to reach the high C in the harmony in both sections. If your hand is big enough you might be able to reach it without straying from first position.

DID YOU EVER SEE THE DEVIL UNCLE JOE? *(harmony)*

Paul Warren (a long-time member of the Flatt and Scruggs band), Kenny Baker (then of the Bill Monroe group), and Curly Ray Cline (of Ralph Stanley's band) jam at a festival. Their garb and lack of facial expression identify their efforts as a bluegrass piece. On the right Roy Lee Centers and Joe Stuart lend guitar support. (photo: Phil Zimmerman)

FIRE ON THE MOUNTAIN *(melody)*

This tune is sometimes played at wild tempos. This version is arranged for the repetitive rhythmic bowing known as the single, simple or Nashville shuffle. <u>The first note after each slur should be accented.</u>

To avoid the ma7 note (here G$\sharp$ or C$\sharp$) in the harmony, some fourths intervals are used as in measures 1, 2 and 4. Try adding open A and D string drones to the harmony in both sections. In the 2nd and 6th measures of the harmony, fiddlers often opt for the easier B note instead of C natural.

In the harmony of the first section you might shift hand position one note earlier than indicated by fingering the F$\sharp$ with your third finger on the A string.

FIRE ON THE MOUNTAIN *(harmony)*

GOLDEN SLIPPERS *(melody)*

Country fiddlers probably will pick "Golden Slippers" for a first double fiddle number with a new partner. It is the tune that is always being played in the saloon scene of every Western movie. Some play this in the key of A. The first double stop in the harmony serves to ease the starkness of the fourth interval that would sound without the added B note. The purpose of the last double stop is to supply a full, fat chord on which to end the chorus.

GOLDEN SLIPPERS *(harmony)*

GOODBYE LIZA JANE *(melody)*

This is another tune that sounds great with a mix of single shuffles and Georgia bows. It comes from the Bob Wills repertoire through Bobby Hicks's great fiddle album "Texas Crapshooter" on County Records. In the second section of the harmony you can omit the lower notes of the double stops. The tune belongs to a play-party with lyrics along the lines of:

> *"Black your boots and make them shine,*
> *A goodbye, a goodbye,*
> *Block your boots and make them shine,*
> *Goodbye Liza Jane."*

GOODBYE LIZA JANE *(harmony)*

HARVEST HOME HORNPIPE *(melody)*

When hornpipes are played in the Old Country, pairs of eighth notes are usually phrased as dotted eighth-sixteenth, instead of the 50-50 split of the beat notated here. However in the United States hornpipes are usually played and phrased as hoedowns. Canada has not yet made up its mind.

HARVEST HOME HORNPIPE *(harmony)*

JUNE APPLE *(melody)*

Try single shuffle and Georgia bow patterns. The first two measures of G have some fourth intervals for that old timey sound. The harmony is a good candidate for transposing down an octave.

26

JUNE APPLE (harmony)

LA CASSINE SPECIAL *(melody)*

This is a famous cajun breakdown *a la* Louisiana. In the melody it is *de rigeur* to add open A string drones over the D chord and open E and A string drones over the A chords.

In this *genre* of music the harmony fiddle (the *segoneur*) traditionally plays a repetitive rhythmic shuffle that defines the chord progression and employs open string drones. It is not a parallel harmony like most of the other arrangements in this book. *Sacre bleu!* The "hammer-on" slur of the first two notes followed by repetitive pitches make up the basic "cajun shuffle." *Zut alors!* Remember to give a strong accent on the second and fourth beats of each shuffle. This effect can make your playing quite danceable. *Formidable!*

Typically the second fiddle also bows two strings. You may add open A string drones to the D chord measures, fingered E and open A notes to the A chord measures, and either G$^{\sharp}$ or B over the E7 chords, *n'est-ce pas?* The pick up measures may be unaccompanied or, if you so choose, continue the A chord form of the harmony from the last measure of this arrangement. I learned this from a version by Michael Doucet. *C'est la vie. C'est si bon. Au revoir.*

LA CASSINE SPECIAL *(harmony)*

LIBERTY (melody)

14

As is typical in double fiddle arrangements of this tune, the basic melody has been changed in the first D and G measures to ease harmonization. In the first measure the D notes are usually played as A's and in the third measure the D notes might be B's.

Experiment with the first and fifth measures of the second section of the harmony with and without the double stops.

LIBERTY (harmony)

MUDDY ROADS *(melody)*

In the fourth measure of the harmony, the second D note can be played as a C♯. The first is needed to help establish the D chord (at least to my ears).

This setting sounds best with some single shuffles and Georgia bows. I prefer playing the first section in unison and breaking into harmony in the second section.

MUDDY ROADS (harmony)

Andy Williams and Dave Milefsky get down (with unidentified fiddleress in the background) at Glenn Smith's festival in Elizabeth, West Virginia in 1973. Their garb leads me to believe that they are partaking in an old time fiddling ritual. (photo: Carl Fleischauer)

OLD FRENCH *(melody)*

"Old French" is a Canadian tune that is a favorite at contra dances. In measure 4 of the harmony of the second section, I chose an A note instead of the G (which is the expected third interval above the melody) because of the relative ease of fingering. Both notes are part of an A7 chord.

OLD FRENCH *(harmony)*

OLD JAW BONE *(melody)*

This minstrel-derived tune has some wild lyrics.

> *"Jaw bone walk and jaw bone talk,*
> *and jaw bone eat with a knife and fork.*
> *I put my jaw bone on the fence,*
> *I ain't seen nothing of my jaw bone since.*
>
> *Old jaw bone, Jimmy get along,*
> *Here comes daddy with the new shoes on.*
> *Old jaw bone, Jimmy get along,*
> *Here comes daddy with the red dress on."*

Say what?

OLD JAW BONE *(harmony)*

OLD JOE CLARK *(melody)*

This arrangement sounds better with three fiddles than with two. In the measure of G I decided that
it sounded weird for all three parts to go up a scale step at the same moment, so I had "harmony no.
2" stay stationary. In the first measure I used similar reasoning in "harmony no. 1." You might prefer
substituting a G natural for the second A note of that measure.

OLD JOE CLARK (*harmony 1*)

OLD JOE CLARK (*harmony 2*)

RED HAIRED BOY *(melody)*

"Red Haired Boy," also called "Little Beggar Boy" and "Guilderoy," shows little of its Irish heritage except the A to G chord progression. This is a good set up for Georgia bow patterns.

RED HAIRED BOY *(harmony)*

TEXAS QUICK STEP *(melody)*

This arrangement works well as a polka. It is based on a setting by Bill Monroe's Blue Grass Boys.

TEXAS QUICK STEP (*harmony*)

Three of the top contest fiddlers in the New England and Canadian circuit, outstanding in their field. Left to right: Rebecca Koehler, Sarah Michaels and Gretchen Koehler. (photo: Hank Haley)

TURKEY IN THE STRAW *(melody)*

Try single shuffle and Georgia bow patterns. What would a fiddle book be without something about barnyard biota?

TURKEY IN THE STRAW *(harmony)*

TWO FRIENDS QUADRILLE *(melody)*

A tune from the New England contra repertoire courtesy of The Deseret String Band.

TWO FRIENDS QUADRILLE *(harmony)*

WEAVE AND WAY *(melody)*

This is not a breakdown. Play at a loping tempo. This fiddle tune entered the bluegrass scene by way of resonator guitarist, Tut Taylor. The slides supply a bluegrass-ey atmosphere. You might try the harmony an octave lower.

WEAVE AND WAY (*harmony*)

WOODCHOPPER'S REEL *(melody)*

This Canadian tune was popularized in the States by Joe Pancerzewski, a fine fiddler from the northwest. If you play the first section harmony an octave down, the F♯ will be out of the range of your violin. You might substitute a low A note.

WOODCHOPPER'S REEL (harmony)

WALTZES AND OTHER SLOW TUNES

DANISH WALTZ *(melody)*

Scandinavian double fiddle tunes tend to have less parallel third harmonies than their American counterparts. There may be a connection between the low temperatures and their fondness for somber minor settings.

DANISH WALTZ (harmony)

FINNISH WALTZ *(melody)*

It is even colder in Finland than Denmark, and the settings get even gloomier.

FINNISH WALTZ *(harmony)*

HOMECOMING WALTZ *(melody)*

The basis of this arrangement is a 1941 recording by Bill Boyd's western swing band. A full transcription of their double fiddles can be found in my "Western Swing Fiddle" book.

The low harmony 2 jumps above the lead in section three. Play the staccato notes very short and near the frog.

56

HOMECOMING WALTZ *(harmony 1)*

HOMECOMING WALTZ *(harmony 2)*

Two of the greatest harmony and double stop players in the history of commercial country music, Buddy Spicher on the left and Dale Potter jamming at one of Buddy's get-togethers in the late 1970's. Steve Chapman and Doug Green (Ranger Doug of Riders in the Sky) accompany on guitar. (photo: Earl Spielman)

MEMORY WALTZ by Howdy Forrester *(melody)*

This became a classic fiddle tune the moment Howdy Forrester first recorded it around 1960. Howdy was the doyen of Nashville hoedown fiddlers in the 1960's and '70's. The double stops in the melody section are a challenge to even experienced players. I decided that writing a harmony part might help neutralize any sour misadventures.

Because of these double stops, the harmony supplies mostly the missing note of the triads in section 2. As a result that part is not very melodic, but it sounds great when played with the lead. I especially relish the few double double stops and contrary motion riffs the harmony supplies here.

For a change-of-pace, section 3 is played in unison. Fall back into harmonies when you return to the funny sign at measure 50.

MEMORY WALTZ *(harmony)*

NORWEGIAN WALTZ (melody)

This entry proves that Scandinavians can occasionally be merry, or that Norway has some warm spells.

Jam session at the 1973 Rosine, Kentucky bluegrass festival with Ray Cline and Kenny Baker on double fiddles. Bill Monroe is singing and playing mandolin. (photo: Carl Fleischauer)

NORWEGIAN WALTZ (*harmony*)

Tracy Schwartz and Mike Seegar at the Brandywine, Pennsylvania (now in Delaware) old time music festival in 1974. They were members of The New Lost City Ramblers, a group that introduced Southeastern old time music to several generations of urban audiences. (photo: Carl Fleischauer)

OLD MADEIRA WALTZ *(melody)*

This haunting waltz is based on a version by Hugh Farr of The Sons of the Pioneers. Play the slides lazily, even slyly.

OLD MADEIRA WALTZ *(harmony)*

SI BHEAG SI MHOR *(melody)*

This pretty waltz is from Ireland. The title is Gaelic for "So Big, So Little." The natural symbol in parentheses can be used instead of the sharp in the key signature.

SI BHEAG SI MHOR *(harmony)*

SITTING ON TOP OF THE WORLD (melody)
Slow Blues Version

Compare this slow country blues version to the bluegrass one later in the book. The slides are integral to the feel of this arrangement. Experiment with different lengths and speeds.

SITTING ON TOP OF THE WORLD (harmony)

Bob Potts and Walt Koken fiddle along with Mac Benford on banjo and Doug Dorshug on guitar at Brandywine, Pennsylvania in 1974. Jenny Cleland on bass is mostly hidden. As the Highwoods String Band they were important northern revivalists of southern old time music for over a decade. They added many microphones to the instrumentation of this genre. Notice the stances of the fiddlers in particular - choking up on the bow with knees akimbo and mouths agape. Their bodies tilt to the right because they were born and raised on the eastern side of a mountain. (photo: Carl Fleischauer)

STAR OF THE COUNTY DOWN *(melody)*

If you are going to learn just one slow Irish tune, this is the most well known of the lot. If the parenthetical Em chords are played, substitute an E note for the D in the second harmony.

STAR OF THE COUNTY DOWN (*harmony 1*)

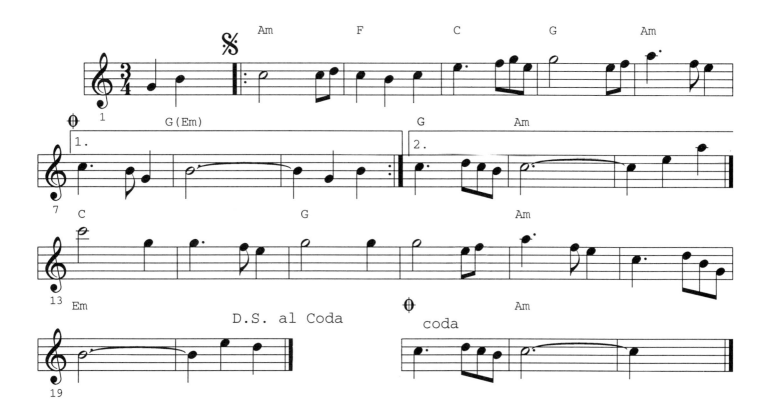

STAR OF THE COUNTY DOWN (*harmony 2*)

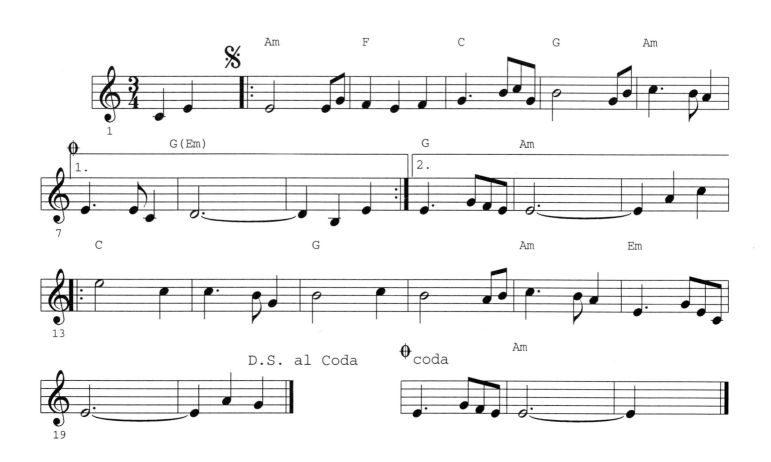

SWEDISH WALKING TUNE *(melody)*

Harmonized fiddle tunes are the rule instead of the exception in Sweden. The melody is usually the highest pitched line, as in this wedding march. The harmony switches between a third and a sixth below the lead. This is one of the most overplayed tunes in the Swedish repertoire.

SWEDISH WALKING TUNE (*harmony*)

TABLEAU CLOG DANCE (melody)

This oddity is a version of a somewhat Canadian dance as recorded by a Western swing ensemble. I learned this from the playing of Carol Hubbard and Kenneth Pitts with Bill Boyd's Cowboy Ramblers band.

The original version was arranged pretty loosely and I have made some minor changes in the harmony to make it a bit more consonant. Yet the relaxed feel of the recording remains, reflected in measures 1, 5 and 6. Play this at about 120 beats per minute on your metronome. Try to do the shag or monkey or other disco steps to this tune's infectious rhythm.

TABLEAU CLOG DANCE (*harmony*)

TOMBIGBEE WALTZ *(melody)*

This tune is named for the Tombigbee River in Alabama. I have tried a bit of contrary motion in the last measure of D7 and after each second repetition. "Tombigbee Waltz" is nice and easy and it sounds good. The perfect combination. I learned this from a Rounder recording by James Bryan.

TOMBIGBEE WALTZ *(harmony)*

Jam session at a New England fiddlers contest. Among the participants are, from the left, Hank Haley, Dan Brooks, Ivan Richards, Rebecca Koehler, unidentified (in rear), Leo LeBlanc, Bob Christopher, Nicki Maranchie, and Sarah Michaels.

WAYFARING STRANGER *(melody)*

Play this sad song as dirge-like as you wish. One of the notes of each of the double stops may be omitted.

"I am a poor, wayfaring stranger,
Travelling through this world alone."

WAYFARING STRANGER *(harmony)*

BLUEGRASS TUNES

CARELESS LOVE *(melody)*

This old tune makes for a pleasant, medium paced bluesy arrangement. The phrasing imitates the contour of the lyrics, but some liberties have been taken with the basic melody. Check out the classic Bill Monroe-type tag.

CARELESS LOVE (harmony)

Left to right: Stacy Phillips, Jim Tolles and Kenny Kosek as part of Breakfast Special rip into a triple fiddle chorus of Merle Haggard's country hit, "The Bottle Let Me Down." Also pictured are Roger Mason on bass (partially hidden), Chris Ditson on drums, and Andy Statman on guitar. Sound man (and banjoist) Eddie Adcock, in the foreground, wonders where the caterwauling is coming from. – It comes from my microphone. (photo: Phil Zimmerman)

IN THE PINES *(melody)*

This arrangement is based on the old Bill Monroe recording of this tune. He has always been partial to keys with three, four and even five sharps. The fiddles should moan like a cold wind blowing through a dark forest. Play very slowly.

IN THE PINES *(harmony)*

86

LITTLE MAGGIE *(melody)*

Play this old tune very fast. The slides are integral to the bluesy feel of this solo. It makes a great break if you know someone who sings as high as Bill Monroe who inspired me to do this in the key of B. Generations of tyro bluegrassers have damaged their vocal chords straining to hit pitches far out of their range in vain attempts to imitate Big Mon.

LITTLE MAGGIE *(harmony)*

R.K. SPECIAL by Stacy Phillips *(melody)*

"R. K. Special" is a high speed bluegrass number that sounds best with a five string banjo rolling like mad through the first two sections. This helps keep the energy up through the relatively long bow portions of section one. The second part should have a bit of a "chugging engine" feel. Even the eighth notes should be a bit staccato. Play that near the frog to minimize the tonal quality and maximize the percussive. The double stop slide should be slow, taking up almost the entire duration of the half note. In measure 2 of the harmony, the G note may be played sharp or natural. It was written with harmony in mind, and so sounds a bit dull without the second line. The latter helps smooth the dissonance of the lead line in section two. End by adding an extra second section after section three.

by Stacy Phillips © Southern Melody Publishing

R.K. SPECIAL *(harmony)*

SITTING ON TOP OF THE WORLD *(melody)*

Bluegrass Version

Play this uptempo. Compare this to the slow blues version on page72. The A note with the sharp in parentheses may be played natural. The stacatto notes should be "chunked" near the frog. The last two measures contain another classic bluegrass tag.

SITTING ON TOP OF THE WORLD (*harmony*)

Triple fiddles on a 1969 version of "Brownskin Gal" for Kapp Records. Left to right: Tommy Jackson (one of the creators of "roots" commercial country fiddling), Johnny Gimble (perhaps the greatest of all western swing fiddlers) and Bob Wills (leader of the most popular western swing group). (photo: Charles Townsend Collection)

TRAIN 45 (melody)

This is based on the way I remember hearing Kenny Baker and Joe Stuart play it in Bill Monroe's band in the 1970's. The slides are integral to the feel of this arrangement. It is filled with the long notes of a train whistle and the rolling rhythm of a speeding steam engine. Adding a banjo helps. In the harmony an A♯ is preferable to the notated open A strings, but at the fast tempo of this piece that fingering can be too demanding to be worth the trouble to play cleanly. The high A naturals are blues notes.

TRAIN 45 (harmony)

John Morris and Wilson Douglas strike a typical pose in the parking area of a festival in Cloe, West Virginia in 1973. Douglas has recorded a few fiddle albums documenting the unique style and repertoire of his home state. The "recreation vehicle" in the background is de riguer *at festivals. (photo: Carl Fleischauer)*

93

WATERMELON ON THE VINE *(melody)*

Bill Monroe and the Blue Grass Boys used to kick off their shows with one very fast chorus of this tune. This is typical of Monroe's taste in double fiddles - many long notes (with a rolling banjo filling up the spaces in the background) and occasional bursts of quick phrases.

Play the introductory notes very short. The ending is another typical Monroe arrangement.

> *"Hambone am sweet, chicken am good,*
> *Rabbit is so very, very fine.*
> *Give me, oh give me, oh how I wish you would,*
> *That watermelon hanging on that vine."*

WATERMELON ON THE VINE *(harmony)*

JIGS

BISHOP OF BANGOR *(melody)*

The accidental sharps may be played natural. If the accompanist plays the F# diminished, the first harmony note should be D# instead of E natural.

BISHOP OF BANGOR *(harmony)*

BLACK NAG (melody)

You can play Em instead of E7 by switching the G♯'s to G naturals. Try using F♯ instead of F♮ in the harmonies. You might prefer the cut of this jib.

BLACK NAG *(harmony)*

99

THE CONNAUGHTMAN'S RAMBLES *(melody)*

THE CONNAUGHTMAN'S RAMBLES *(harmony)*

COWBOY JIG *(melody)*

COWBOY JIG (harmony)

THE IRISH WASHERWOMAN *(melody)*

To avoid upper positions, I changed the octave of the second section harmony.

THE IRISH WASHERWOMAN *(harmony)*

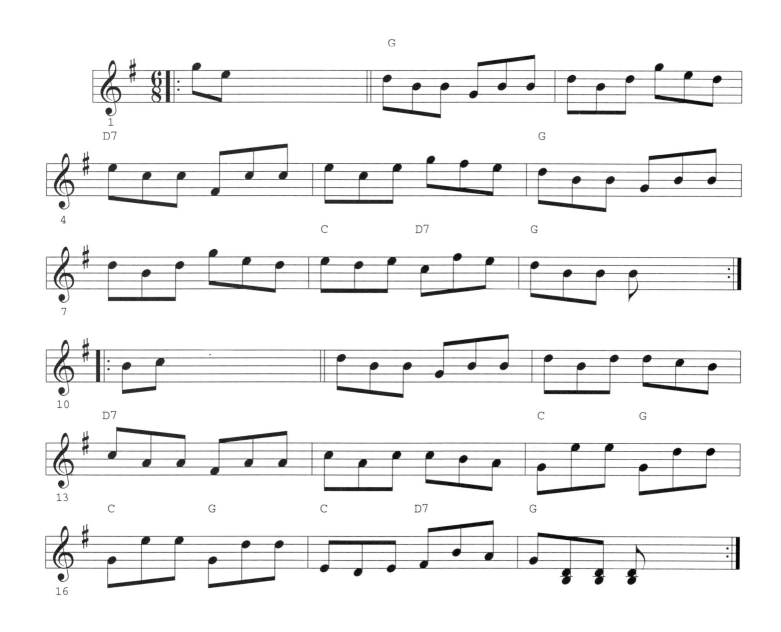

JOYS OF WEDLOCK (*melody*)

On the C chords, you might prefer C notes to the B notes I notated in the harmony. Similarly, in the fifth measure of the second section of the harmony, the F♯ can be replaced by another G note.

106

JOYS OF WEDLOCK (harmony)

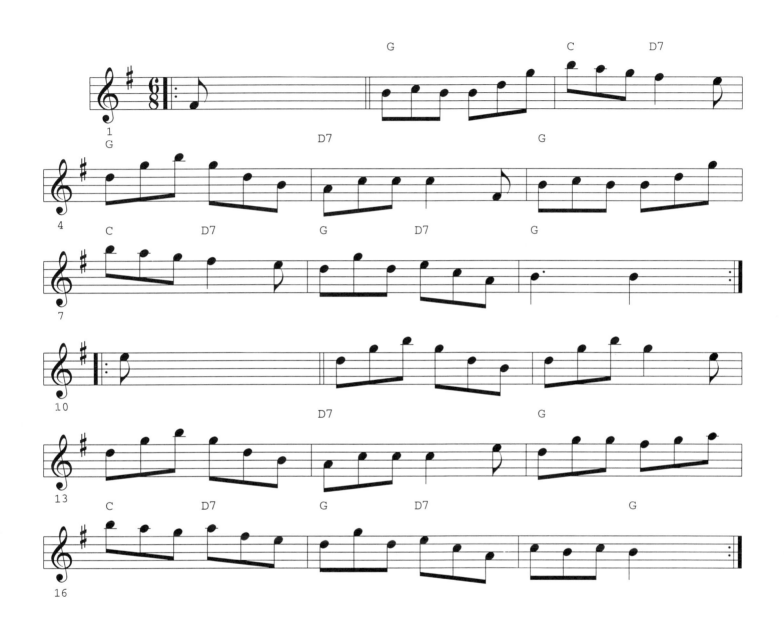

THOMPSON'S JIG *(melody)*

If you tremble at the thought of playing so many high notes in the harmony, rewrite it one octave down. I think that sounds a bit low, but it is preferable to avoiding this fine melody. If you do transpose, you also should be able to compose a third part between the melody and low harmony. I like to play the whole second section of the harmony in second position. If this is a problem, you might try to mix in some third and first position.

This is based on a version by Canada's Angus Chisolm.

THOMPSON'S JIG *(harmony)*

TOBIN'S JIG *(melody)*

TOBIN'S JIG (*harmony*)

RAGS, JIGS, SWING TUNES, ETC.

BULLY OF THE TOWN (melody)

In the first measure of the second section the chord is established with a G as the first note of the harmony. I then revert to intervals of a third for the rest of the measure.

BULLY OF THE TOWN (*harmony*)

GRAN TEXAS *(melody)*

This cajun melody was borrowed by Hank Williams for his great hit, "Jambalaya." Here it is arranged in commercial country style. The shuffle in the last two measures can continue as a backup during the vocal, or can end when the lyrics begin.

GRAN TEXAS *(harmony)*

JESSE POLKA *(melody)*

This Mexican polka, originally titled "Jesusito en Chihuahua" is now a standard of western fiddling. The first part is often played pizzicato. You might enjoy an F♮ instead of F♯ in measure 12 of the harmony.

JESSE POLKA (harmony)

PEOR ES NADA *(melody)*

This is a three section Mexican polka. The lead is always the higher pitched violin. In the second part the second violin is not a harmony, but a sort of bass line.

The order of sections is 1-2-1-3-1. When section 3 is repeated, play it an octave higher.

PEOR ES NADA (*harmony*)

121

RAINBOW (melody)

This was a staple of both the western swing and bluegrass repertoires with roots in the polite parlor music of the late nineteenth century. The arrangement needs both harmonies to sound right. Play this at a medium tempo. The first section swings and the second is more lyrical.

RAINBOW (*harmony 1*)

RAINBOW (*harmony 2*)

Johnny Gimble and Mark O'Connor twinning on Gimble's composition, "Fiddlin' Around" in Oregon in 1995. (photo: Jim Bradley)

REDWING *(melody)*

This is often played as a hoedown but is more properly a polka. The harmony switches from above the melody to below when the latter jumps up in the introduction to the second section. Woody Guthrie used this as the melody for his "Union Maid."

REDWING (harmony)

SILVER BELLS *(melody)*

In the first section the harmony is below the lead. It jumps above for the second section with a swing-y rhythm. This is another staple of the Western swing repertoire. It is sometimes performed without the modulation.

SILVER BELLS (harmony)

SNOW DEER *(melody)*

In the first measure the C's can be played natural or sharp. I don't know what a snow deer is, but I guess it isn't a reindeer.

SNOW DEER *(harmony)*

SPANISH TWO STEP *(melody)*

This is taken from the Bob Wills repertoire. The repeats have a slightly skewed phrasing, with a chord change at an unexpected moment. Wills was fond of this type of metric oddness, which must have caused much merriment in The Texas Playboys' rhythm section.

SPANISH TWO STEP (harmony)

STEALING HOME *(melody)*

This is a country swing number with some interesting double stop harmonies. The chord in the last measure is an "augmented G7" (a major triad with the 5th note raised a half step, plus a flat 7 note, here D♯ and F natural, respectively).

The playing order of sections is: 1-1-2-1(with the second ending). Swing the 1/8's. I learned this from one of the old timers of the Connecticut country scene, Ron Kehoe.

134

STEALING HOME *(harmony)*

TAKING OFF (*melody*)

This is based on the tune by Bob Dunn, great steel guitarist for Milton Brown and His Musical Brownies, the original western swing band. Most of this arrangement is the work of two fiddling friends of mine, Tom Hagymasi and Kenny Kosek. I especially like the doubled double stops that pepper this piece. But be careful. It is hard—wicked hard.It was recorded (along with "Homecoming Waltz") on an old album of mine, "All Old Friends" on Revonah Records. You might still find a copy in the cut-out bin of your local "Everything For A Dollar" store.

The harmony switches back-and-forth from above to below the melody. Some of the melody really needs the harmony to sound right. Swing the eighth notes like crazy.

The momentary switch to unison about three-quarters of the way through this piece is an old swing technique.

TAKING OFF *(harmony)*

137

WASHINGTON AND LEE SWING (*melody*)

This version comes from the playing of Cliff Bruner and Cecil Brower when members of Milton Brown's western swing band in the mid-1930's. It works well as a polka.

WASHINGTON AND LEE SWING (*harmony*)

YEAR OF THE JUBILO *(melody)*

YEAR OF THE JUBILO
Play this Civil War era tune as a polka.

> *"Old master's run away,*
> *And the darkies stay at home,*
> *Must be now that kingdom's coming,*
> *In the year of Jubilo."*

YEAR OF THE JUBILO (*harmony*)

Left to right: Frank George and Alan Jabbour at a festival in Pipestem, West Virginia in 1973. Both have been important conservators of Southeastern fiddle styles and repertoire. Another fine old time fiddler, Oscar Wright (at left) enjoys the music. (photo: Carl Fleischauer)

Music Theory

This chapter exposes some of the thinking (if I dare be so generous to myself) that goes into the choice of notes in the arrangements in this book. It should enable you to create your own harmony lines. Do not bother memorizing this stuff. You learn it by repeatedly using it as you practice writing harmonies. It becomes easy after just a few tries.

Here are the ground rules. There are twelve pitches (called scale steps) between notes an octave apart. A note an octave above another has twice the frequency of the first pitch, and sounds a lot like the first, especially when played simultaneously. It is the most consonant *interval* (ie. space between two notes). Beginning with "A" the twelve pitch (chromatic) scale is:

A–A♯ (for our purposes, the same as B♭)–B–C–C♯ (D♭)–D–D♯ (E♭)–E–F–F♯ (G♭)–G–G♯ (A♭)–A

The interval between consecutive notes of the chromatic scale is called a *half step* or a *minor second*. An interval of two half steps is a *whole step* or *major second*. There are half steps between B and C and also E and F. Otherwise there are whole steps between the *natural* (not flat, ♭, or sharp, ♯) species of pitches ie., G-A, A-B, C-D etc..

The major scale is a way of dividing an octave into eight *steps*. The intervals between the eight notes (the eighth being an octave above the first) are uneven, either half or whole steps.

TABLE I : THE COMMON MAJOR SCALES IN FIDDLE MUSIC

Scale-Step Numbers →	Whole Step 1	Whole Step 2	Half Step 3	Whole Step 4	Whole Step 5	Whole Step 6	Half Step 7	Whole Step 8	Whole Step 9	Half Step 10	Whole Step 11	Whole Step 12	13
A	A	B	C♯	D	E	F♯	G♯	A	B	C♯	D	E	F♯
B♭	B♭	C	D	E♭	F	G	A	B♭	C	D	E♭	F	G
B	B	C♯	D♯	E	F♯	G♯	A♯	B	C♯	D♯	E	F♯	G♯
C	C	D	E	F	G	A	B	C	D	E	F	G	A
D	D	E	F♯	G	A	B	C♯	D	E	F♯	G	A	B
E	E	F♯	G♯	A	B	C♯	D♯	E	F♯	G♯	A	B	C♯
F	F	G	A	B♭	C	D	E	F	G	A	B♭	C	D
G	G	A	B	C	D	E	F♯	G	A	B	C	D	E

For the comparison of scales in general, numbers are assigned to each scale step as shown in Table I.

You should become familiar with methods of labelling intervals. One is to count the number of steps between two notes. The more common nomenclature is illustrated in Table II. **Count the lower note of the interval as number 1**. Then count the number of letters to the higher note of the interval. So A-C and A-C♯ are both third intervals. A third of 1-1/2 steps is a minor third; one of two steps is a major third. The common intervals and the equivalent number of steps are listed in Table II.

TABLE II : THE COMMON INTERVALS

Lower Note of Interval	Upper Note of Interval	Number of Whole Steps	Name of Interval
A	B♭	½	minor second
A	B	1	major second
A	C	1½	minor (or flatted) third
A	C♯	2	major third
A	D	2½	perfect fourth
A	E♭	3	diminished (or flatted) fifth
A	E	3½	perfect fifth
A	F	4	minor sixth
A	F♯	4½	minor (or flatted) seventh
A	G	5	minor seventh
A	G♯	5½	major seventh
A	A	6	octave
A	B♭	6½	minor (or flatted) ninth
A	B	7	major ninth

"A" is used as the lower note throughout this table, though any note could have been used as a reference point. **The identity of an interval is independent of the scale**. So C-E is a major third whether those notes are the first and third steps of a C scale, the fourth and sixth of a G scale, or the flat third and fifth of an A scale.

For historical reasons the intervals of a fourth and fifth are often called *perfect* and *diminished* instead of major and minor.

The harmonies I choose are often dependent on the accompanying *chords*. Chords are the simultaneous sounding of at least three notes. Almost all chords are built by imposing a series of major and minor third intervals above a fundamental note called the *root* or *tonic* (assigned the number "1") that gives its name to the chord.

In fiddling we generally deal with the **naturally occurring** (or **diatonic**) **chords** of the major scales. ("Naturally occurring" means that the chords contain only notes present in the parent scale.) Start with any note, pick the note up a third interval, then up another third interval and you now have the menu for a three note chord. Looking at the A major scale in Table I, the process boils down to using the first note, skipping the second, using the third skipping the next, etc.:

$$\begin{array}{cccccccc} \textbf{A} & \textbf{B} & \textbf{C♯} & \textbf{D} & \textbf{E} & \textbf{F♯} & \textbf{G♯} & \textbf{A} \\ \textbf{1} & & \textbf{3} & & \textbf{5} & & & \end{array}$$

The 1, 3 and 5 notes are the basic major triad. Table III details the process.

TABLE III: THE NATURALLY OCCURRING THREE-NOTE CHORDS
IN THE KEY OF A WITH THEIR INTERNAL INTERVALS

Chord Recipe	minor third / major third, perfect fifth (E, C♯, A)	major third / minor third, perfect fifth (F♯, D, B)	major third / minor third, perfect fifth (G♯, E, C♯)	minor third / major third, perfect fifth (A, F♯, D)	minor third / major third, perfect fifth (B, G♯, E)	major third / minor third, perfect fifth (C♯, A, F♯)	minor third / minor third, diminished fifth (D, B, G♯)
Chord Symbol	A	Bm	C♯m	D	E	F♯m	G♯°
Chord Name	A major	B minor	C♯ minor	D major	E major	F♯ minor	G♯ diminished
Chord Number	I	II	III	IV	V	VI	VII

Notice that numbers are employed to place a note in a scale, a chord in a progression and to indicate the interval between notes. Try to keep clear which number refers to which quality.

When choosing harmonies the basic approach is to use thirds the same way chords are constructed. This has to be balanced against the need of the harmonies to fit in with the accompanying chord. This last proviso becomes a factor when the melody note is the fifth note of the chord. For example, let's say the melody note is E, to be played over an A chord. Referring to the tables in this chapter, the standard harmony a third interval higher is G♯. As a passing note this harmony is fine. However, if the note has a long duration, or it falls on the first beat of a measure, it often does not sound right (against an A chord). The major seventh note (here G♯) is too jazzy for traditional fiddle music. (On swing numbers it can be just the right sound.)

The alternative is to use the next highest scale note for harmony. That turns out to be the eighth note of the scale (which has the same identity as the first). The resultant fourth interval is not as restful as thirds and sixths but it is usually better than the original choice. (Remember, if G♯/E sounds for just an 1/8 note duration over an A chord, it is acceptable.)

Another strategy is to position the harmony below the melody. For an E note, a C♯ a major third below could be used. When the melody is the highest pitched line, it is relatively easy to switch between thirds and sixths in the low harmony. This can sound awkward when done above the melody because the change is too prominent.

When the melody uses a note outside the chord, again use third intervals as shown in Table III. Whether to use a major or minor third depends upon the parent scale. For example, if the melody calls for a D note, the corresponding harmony would be an F♯ a major third above, even if the accompanying chord is an A. (In a different key the parent scale might call for an F natural, a minor third above. Check Table I.)

It is critical to note that this discussion concerns guidelines not rules. Your ear is the final judge. There certainly are times where fourth, fifth and even second and seventh intervals are just right. Still if you are interested in sounding like a bluegrass or swing player, you must immerse yourself in the music of the masters until your ear has absorbed their language. Then certain choices just sound right, in the same way as a spoken language might. (If you are not interested in any sort of copying, and want to create your own sound, your ear is responsible for creating new guidelines.)

144

For example, in bluegrass it is customary to harmonize the five note of the I and IV chords with the tonic note, pitched a perfect fourth above. The next four statements also apply **specifically to bluegrass** and other blues based music **and** when the harmony is above the melody. For example, in the key of A, and referring to Table III:

1. An E note over an A chord (the I chord) is harmonized with a high A note.
2. An A note over a D chord (the IV chord) is harmonized with a high D.
3. A B note over an E chord (the V chord) is harmonized with D, a minor third above.
4. The ♭7 note is occasionally used to harmonize the fifth note of the I and IV chords, even though it is outside the scale. This gives a blues effect to a bluegrass line. That would be G ♮/ E over an A chord and C ♮/A over a D chord. (See the entries in the bluegrass section for many examples.)

****

Excepting the swing and Scandinavian entries, it is standard for the harmony to be a third above the melody. Those specific styles usually have the harmony below the lead. This ordering tends to let the melody stick out more than the alternative. It is also easier to switch unobtrusively between third and sixth intervals. However there is no rule about this stuff and I used all the permutations.

Infrequently I applied counter motion (i.e. the harmony and melody move in opposite directions). This is not the typical sound for tradition-based music, in which the harmony usually follows a parallel motion i.e., follows the up and down contour of the melody. These moves sometimes have dissonances along the way, but always wind up with a harmonious interval.

I do not employ any classical counterpoint because the sound does not seem appropriate in these genres to me (and because I do not know how).

The same thinking that has just been outlined is also employed to select double stops for one fiddler and for vocal duets.

Minute thirteen of a marathon rendition of "June Apple." Front, left to right: Stacy Phillips, Will Welling, Jane Rothfield; back, left to right: Tom Hagymasi, Dave Howard, Sue Sterngold, Bill Christopherson. (photo: Georgia Sheron)

Other Fiddle Books

All happen to be written by me. (Ahem) Write to me care of Mel Bay Publications or at 36 Cromwell Drive, Monroe, NY 10950 for further information.

1. **Bluegrass Fiddle Styles** - careful transcriptions of over 60 of the most influential bluegrass solos...Chubby Wise, Benny Martin, Vassar Clements, Richard Greene, Bobby Hicks, Paul Warren, Scotty Stoneman, Kenny Baker, Jimmy Buchanan, Byron Berline, etc. plus a few double fiddle numbers ...the book that tells the whole truth...includes analyses and historical background with **60 minute accompanying cassette**

2. **Mark O'Connor - The Championship Years** - meticulous transcriptions of Mark's trend-setting performances at fiddle contests...written with Mark's help...major interviews and detailed analyses...the most influential fiddle style of the past fifteen years

3. **Western Swing Fiddle** - the complete scoop on this music... transcriptions and analyses of the great solos and tunes with many double fiddle entries...interviews with Johnny Gimble, Joe Holley, Cliff Bruner, Bobby Bruce...the music of Bob Wills, J.R. Chatwell, Hugh Farr, Keith Coleman, Louis Tierney, Holley, Bruner, Bruce, Spade Cooley, Jesse Ashlock, Cecil Brower etc., and a whole chapter of Johnny Gimble solos...accompanying **90 minute cassette** includes 20 tunes omitted from the book (for reasons of space) **with their transcriptions** in a booklet

4. **The Complete Country Fiddler** - how to create authentic licks and solos in the major modern fiddle styles of blues, swing, bluegrass and commercial country....300 examples plus many full solos with complete explanations...eleven major interviews with top professional players including Buddy Spicher, Mark O'Connor, Benny Martin, Vassar Clements, John Hartford, Dale Potter and the top studio cats from Nashville and New York...chapter on amplification of the fiddle and a review of the current electric set ups...in depth looks at Tommy Jackson, Dale Potter and Johnny Gimble... **with 60 minute accompanying CD**

5. **Beginning Fiddle** - getting started from scratch, with standard repertoire and correct bowings in different keys

6. **Old Time Southern Fiddle Case Tunebook** - 50 tunes from the various southern traditions...with bowings...designed to fit in your fiddle case

7. **Hot Licks For Bluegrass Fiddle** - over 450 bluegrass licks and how to apply them to your own solos...sections on double stops, upper positions, kickoffs, tags, fills, and a whole chapter on the ins and outs of "Orange Blossom Special"...includes **insert record**

8. **The Phillips Collection of Traditional American Fiddle Tunes** - an unprecedented compendium of over 1350 American fiddle tunes...in two volumes (the first - hoedowns and reels, the second - rags, blues, listening pieces, polkas, hornpipes, jigs, waltzes etc.)...each entry based on the playing of an outstanding fiddler (over 300 represented) with multiple versions of many tunes...bowing, fingering and chordal accompaniment included

9. **Beginning Fiddle Solos** - Easy fiddle tunes for rookies...with accompanying recording and explanation of fingering and reading rhythm notation

****

"Fiddler" magazine (P.O. Box 125, Los Altos, CA 94022) is a recently introduced publication that deals with all aspects of the art. The first few issues have included some interesting columns on bowing.

"Devil's Box" (305 Stella Drive, Madison, AL 35758) mostly focuses on American southern and mid-west fiddle styles. Like "Fiddler," each issue has some fiddle tune transcriptions.